An Introductory Small-Group Bible Study

Great Women of the Bible

Jochebed, Miriam, Deborah, Ruth, and Hannah

CONCORDIA PUBLISHING HOUSE • SAINT LOUIS

Contents

Hymnal Key

LSB = Lutheran Service Book
ELH = Evangelical Lutheran Hymnary
CW = Christian Worship
LW = Lutheran Worship
LBW = Lutheran Book of Worship
TLH = The Lutheran Hymnal

About This Series

Do you realize how often women are mentioned in the Bible? Do names like Eve, Sarah, Deborah, Ruth, Esther, Mary the mother of Jesus, Anna, Mary and Martha, Lydia, and Eunice and Lois sound familiar? They should. These are only a few of the great women mentioned in Holy Scripture.

The Bible not only gives us the names of these great women, but also describes their sorrows and joys, their defeats and victories, their intense private moments and important public duties. In contrast to the inaccurate myth that the Bible is an antiquated piece of antiwoman (misogynistic) literature, the Bible portrays women as God's creatures, different yet fully equal with men, fallen in sin yet redeemed by the precious blood of the Lamb.

In addition to sharing the thoughts, dreams, words, and deeds of women in the past, the Bible also provides helpful instruction for women of today. It encourages thrift and industry (Proverbs 31:10–31), teaches about healthy relationships between husbands and wives (Ephesians 5:22–33; Colossians 3:18–19), provides instruction in the relationship between older and younger women (Titus 2:3–5), celebrates the equality in diversity among believers (Galatians 3:28–29), and extols the important and varied roles women play in the partnership of the Gospel (Philippians 4:3).

Women can learn much about themselves in the Bible. But it would be a mistake to assume that what the Bible teaches about women is of no importance to men. In His Word, God unfolds for the believer both true womanhood and true manhood as He designed them, so that both sexes are affirmed in their equality and in their differences as God created them.

In this series, we cannot learn all there is to know about every great woman of the Bible. However, as we study God's Word we can learn much about ourselves and our gracious Lord and how He worked in the lives of the great women of the Bible.

Suggestions for Small-Group Participants

1. Before you begin, spend some time in prayer asking God to strengthen your faith through a study of His Word. The Scriptures were written so that we might believe in Jesus Christ and have life in His name (John 20:31).

2. Even if you are not the small-group leader, prior to the meeting take some time to look over the session, read the Bible verses, and answer the questions.

3. As a courtesy to others, be sure to arrive at each session on time.

4. Be an active participant. The leader is there to facilitate group discussion, not give a lecture.

5. Avoid dominating the conversation by answering each question or by giving unnecessarily long answers. Avoid the temptation to not share at all.

6. Treat anything shared in your group as confidential until you have asked and received permission to share it outside of the group. Treat information about others outside of your group as confidential until you have asked and received permission to share it inside of your group.

7. Realize that some participants may be new to the group or new to the Christian faith. Help them to feel welcomed and comfortable.

8. Affirm other participants when you can. If another participant offers what you perceive to be a "wrong" answer, ask the Holy Spirit to guide that person to seek the correct answer from God's Word.

9. Keep in mind that the questions are discussion starters. Don't be afraid to ask additional questions that relate to the session. Avoid getting the group off track.

10. If you feel comfortable doing so, now and then volunteer to pray either at the beginning or at the conclusion of the session.

Suggestions for Small-Group Leaders

1. Before you begin, spend some time in prayer asking God to strengthen your faith through a study of His Word. The Scriptures were written so that we might believe in Jesus Christ and have life in His name (John 20:31). Also, pray for participants by name.

2. See the Leader Guide at the back of this study. It will help guide you in discovering the truths of God's Word. It is not, however, exhaustive nor are is it designed to be read aloud during your session.

3. Prior to your meeting, familiarize yourself with each session by reviewing the session material, reading the Bible passages, and answering the questions in the spaces provided. Your familiarity with the session will give you confidence as you lead the group.

4. As a courtesy to participants, begin and end each session on time.

5. Have a Bible dictionary or similar resource handy in order to look up difficult or unfamiliar names, words, and places. Ask participants to help you in this task. Be sure that each participant has a Bible and a study guide.

6. Ask for volunteers to read introductory paragraphs and Bible passages. A simple "thank you" will encourage them to volunteer again.

7. See your role as a conversation facilitator rather than as a lecturer. Don't be afraid to give participants time to answer questions. By name, thank each participant who answers, then ask for other participants. For example, you may say, "Thank you, Maggie. Would anyone else like to share?"

8. Now and then, summarize aloud what the group has learned by studying God's Word.

9. Keep in mind that the questions provided are discussion starters. Allow participants to ask questions that relate to the session. However, keep discussions on track with the session.

10. Everyone is a learner! If you don't know the answer to a question, simply tell participants that you need time to look at more

Scripture passages, or to ask your pastor, director of Christian education, or other lay leader. You can provide an answer at the next session.

11. Begin each session with prayer. Conclude each session with prayer. Ask for volunteers for these duties, and thank them for their participation. A suggested hymn is included at the end of each session. You may choose another hymn or song if you wish.

12. Encourage participants to read or reread the Scripture passages provided at the end of the session and, as they have time, to commit passages to memory.

❦
Jochebed and Miriam

When it comes to famous people, it is always interesting to know something about their parents—especially their mothers! Most people owe the success they experience later in life to their mothers. The influence, encouragement, and direction mothers offer their young children are very important. God gave Moses a wonderful mother. Moses' sister also played an important role in his life, and some of his success was undoubtedly due to her loyalty to him. Thanks be to God for mothers, sisters, and other female family members and friends that God gives us to help, to encourage, and to guide!

Jochebed, a Loving and Resourceful Mother

Moses' mother was named Jochebed (YOKE-uh-bed; Hebrew: "The LORD is glory") (Exodus 6:20; Numbers 26:59a). God gave Jochebed a strong faith that enabled her to do some extraordinary things on behalf of her son (Hebrews 11:23). *189 U*

1. Besides Moses, her youngest child, who were Jochebed's other two children (Numbers 26:59)? *229*

Husband - Aaaran
Children - Aaron, Miriam, Moses

2. Because of Hebrew "overpopulation" in Egypt, Pharaoh ruled that every Hebrew boy had to be killed (Exodus 1:22). What courageous plan did Jochebed devise to save Moses' life (Exodus 2:2–4)?

3. God directed events so that Jochebed had her son returned to her (Exodus 2:5–9). What opportunity did she have to positively influence her son? What lesson can we learn from Jochebed?

She nursed & raised Moses, She all lots of opportunity

Miriam, a Leader of Women

No doubt Jochebed had a godly influence over her other children, including her eldest child, Miriam (see Exodus 2:4; 7:7). Let's learn about Moses' sister.

4. How did Miriam show her love and concern for her baby brother (Exodus 2:4–9)? How did she show that she was reliable, respectful, and quick-witted at a young age?

5. Besides faith, God gave Miriam many gifts, including prophecy, poetry and music, and leadership among women (see Exodus 15:20–21; Micah 6:4). What gifts has God given you to serve His people? *1383*

6. God disciplined Miriam for grumbling against Moses and pitting her gifts against his (Numbers 12:1–16). How should we relate to other believers exercising their gifts in the proper way (see 1 Corinthians 12:21–26)? *1763*

One part of the body can't do w/out the other part.

Other Women of That Period

It appears likely that Hebrew women in Jochebed and Miriam's day were physically stronger and thus could bear more children than Egyptian women. The Bible doesn't tell us the reason why.

7. How did the Hebrew midwives prove that they feared God more than earthly rulers (Exodus 1:15–21; see also Acts 5:29)? What are some examples of people demanding us to go against God's Word?

8. In contrast to her father, what admirable traits did Pharaoh's daughter possess (Exodus 1:22; 2:5–10)? In what ways was Moses blessed as her adopted son?

9. Zipporah (zip-PORE-uh) became Moses' wife (Exodus 2:21–22). How did she save her husband's life (4:24–26)? How may Christian wives serve their husbands' spiritual welfare?

10. What important service to the Lord did the women of Israel provide while in the desert (Exodus 35:20–35)? List the opportunities for service women have in your congregation.

11. What legal rights were granted to women because of the complaint of the daughters of Zelophehad (zuh-LOW-fuh-had; Numbers 27:1–11)? How are Christians to go about asking for fair treatment among their peers?

12. Who was the remarkable and courageous Rahab (RAY-hab; Joshua 2; Matthew 1:1, 5; Hebrews 11:31; James 2:25)? How does the Gospel of Jesus Christ liberate us to be all that God has

called us to be (see Galatians 3:26–27; Ephesians 2:8–10; Hebrews 12:1–2)?

Closing Worship

Close by reading or singing together the words of "Song of Moses and Israel" (*LSB* 925).

Refrain: I will sing to the LORD, for He has triumphed gloriously; the horse and his rider He has thrown into the sea.

The LORD is my strength and my song,
    And He has become my salvation;
this is my God, and I will praise Him;
    My father's God, and I will exalt Him.
Refrain

The LORD is a man of war;
    the LORD is His name.
Pharaoh's chariots and his host He cast into the sea,
    and his chosen officers were sunk in the Red Sea.
The floods covered them;
    they went down into the depths like a stone.
Your right hand, O LORD, glorious in power,
    Your right hand, O LORD, shatters the enemy.
Refrain

Who is like You, O LORD, among the gods?
    who is like You, majestic in holiness, awesome in glorious deeds, doing wonders?
You stretched out Your right hand;
    the earth swallowed them.
You have led in Your steadfast love the people whom You have redeemed;
    You have guided them by Your strength to Your holy abode.

You will bring them in and plant them on Your own mountain,

the place, O LORD, which You have made for Your abode,
the sanctuary, O LORD, which Your hands have established.
The LORD will reign forever and ever.
Glory be to the Father and to the Son and to the Holy Spirit;
as it was in the beginning,
is now, and will be forever. Amen.
Refrain

Exodus 15:1–6, 11–13, 17–18 ESV
© 2001 Crossway Bibles

❧

For Daily Bible Reading

Monday: Exodus 1–2
Tuesday: Exodus 3–4
Wednesday: Exodus 14–15
Thursday: Exodus 18–20
Friday: Exodus 35
Saturday: Numbers 12 and 27
Sunday: Hebrews 11
For memorization: Hebrews 11:13, 16, 26

Deborah

So far in this series, we have studied women mentioned in the first six books of the Bible. In the Book of Judges, we meet several women in Israel's history who became prominent from the time of Joshua to Samuel. We will not have time to study the lives of all these women in detail. But if we want to become acquainted with the most important woman of that period, we must study the life of Deborah. Deborah's name means "bee" in Hebrew—and that seems especially fitting. Trusting in her Lord, Deborah proved her industry, intelligence, determination, leadership, and faithfulness on behalf of God's people.

Deborah as a Judge

After the death of Joshua, dark and evil days came upon the children of Israel (see Judges 2:8–15). In spite of their sin, out of His boundless compassion God sent judges, or leaders, to save His people from their enemies (v. 16).

13. God allowed foreign nations to rule His people in order to test His people's obedience (Judges 3:4–7). Who was their chief oppressor at the time of Deborah (4:1–3)?

14. God chose Deborah to lead His people. What do we know about her (Judges 4:4–5)? How would you describe her professional relationship with Barak (buh-ROCK), the commander of the Israelite army (see vv. 6–10)?

15. What important role did Deborah play in an important battle (vv. 14–15)? Another great woman, Jael (jah-EL; Hebrew: "mountain goat") slew Sisera (SIS-er-uh), the commander of Jabin's (JUH-bean) army (vv. 16–22). How did God use a "bee" and a "mountain goat" to preserve for His people the "land of milk and honey"?

16. God, our heavenly Father, strengthens us for the task at hand and works through us to accomplish His purposes (vv. 23–24). How does Deborah serve as a great example of devoted faith in service?

Deborah's Hymn of Victory

In a lengthy hymn, Deborah and Barak praised God for His victory on behalf of Israel (Judges 5). After performing much important public service, Deborah still primarily considered herself a "mother in Israel" (v. 7).

17. Through Deborah, Barak, and the Israelite army, God defeated the Canaanites. What battles has God fought and won for you? If you feel comfortable, share some of those victories with the group.

18. How did Deborah praise Jael (vv. 24–27)? Which of Jael's vocations did Deborah highlight (v. 24)? How does God-given faith enable us to serve in the many vocations God gives us?

Other Women in the Book of Judges

19. Who was Achsah (AHK-sah; Judges 1:12–15)? Why is it permissible to be assertive when asking for what we need?

20. What did Jephthah's (JEFF-thuh) daughter suffer because of her father's rash promise (Judges 11:30–40)? Why is it important to consider the consequences before making any promise?

21. What remarkable experience did Manoah's (muh-NO-uh) wife have (Judges 13)? Who appeared to her (v. 18; see also Isaiah 9:6)? If you feel comfortable, discuss those times when God has strengthened you for a special task.

22. The Lord desired that Samson marry a Philistine woman in spite of his parents' objections. Why (Judges 14:1–20)? Why should we be more concerned about God's will for our lives than the opinions of others?

23. Who was Delilah, and what role did she play in Samson's life (Judges 16:4–21)? Who was to blame for Samson becoming weak and helpless?

24. Micah (MY-kuh; not the prophet by the same name) was not blessed with a faithful mother (Judges 17:2–5). How should Christian children treat their parents (1 Timothy 5:4)?

Closing Worship

Close by reading or singing together the words of "The God of Abraham Praise" (*LSB* 798; *LW* 450; *TLH* 40; *LBW* 544; *ELH* 69).

The God of Abr'ham praise,
    Who reigns enthroned above;
Ancient of everlasting days
    And God of love.
Jehovah, great I AM!
    By earth and heav'n confessed;
I bow and bless the sacred name
    Forever blest.

The God of Abr'ham praise,
    At whose supreme command
From earth I rise and seek the joys
    At His right hand.
I all on earth forsake,
    Its wisdom, fame, and pow'r,
And Him my only portion make,
    My shield and tow'r.

The God of Abr'ham praise,
    Whose all-sufficient grace
Shall guide me all my pilgrim days
    In all my ways.
He deigns to call me friend;
    He calls Himself my God.
And He shall save me to the end
    Through Jesus' blood.

He by Himself has sworn;
   I on His oath depend.
I shall, on eagle wings upborne,
   To heav'n ascend.
I shall behold His face;
   I shall His pow'r adore
And sing the wonders of His grace
   Forevermore.

Though nature's strength decay,
   And earth and hell withstand,
To Canaan's bounds I urge my way
   At His command.
The wat'ry deep I pass,
   With Jesus in my view,
And through the howling wilderness
   My way pursue.

The goodly land I see,
   With peace and plenty blest:
A land of sacred liberty
   And endless rest.
There milk and honey flow,
   And oil and wine abound,
And trees of life forever grow
   With mercy crowned.

There dwells the Lord our king,
   The Lord our righteousness,
Triumphant o'er the world and sin,
   The Prince of Peace.
On Zion's sacred height
   His kingdom He maintains
And glorious with His saints in light
   Forever reigns.

The God who reigns on high
   The great archangels sing,
And "Holy, holy, holy!" cry,
   "Almighty King!

Who was and is the same
   And evermore shall be:
Jehovah, Father, great I AM!
   We worship Thee!"

The whole triumphant host
   Give thanks to God on high.
"Hail, Father, Son, and Holy Ghost!"
   They ever cry.
Hail, Abr'ham's God and mine!
   I join the heav'nly lays:
All might and majesty are Thine
   And endless praise!

Thomas Olivers, (1725–99), alt.
Public domain

For Daily Bible Reading

Monday: Judges 1–3
Tuesday: Judges 4–5
Wednesday: Judges 6–8
Thursday: Judges 11–12
Friday: Judges 13–14
Saturday: Judges 15–16
Sunday: Judges 21
For memorization: 1 Timothy 2:9–13; 1 Corinthians 7:2, 9, 39

~ Ruth

The Book of Ruth contains one of the most moving stories in the Bible. Fiction has never produced a tale of such beauty. The Book of Ruth shows how God works through the lives of seemingly ordinary individuals, people like you and me, in order to bless and preserve His people. As a person, Ruth demonstrates the true beauty of faith-filled devotion to loved ones and selfless service for the good of one's neighbor. Both women and men will find that Ruth is a woman to be loved and admired. Every believer should seek to have a character as noble and beautiful as that of Ruth, the Moabitess, who by God's grace chose to cast her lot with God's people.

Ruth's Loyalty to Naomi

Read Ruth 1:1–5. Ruth lived during the period of the judges. Like Orpah (OR-pah), she was the daughter-in-law of Elimelech (el-LI-melek) and Naomi (nay-OH-me), having married one of their sons.

25. What great sorrow did Ruth experience as a young wife (v. 5)? Do you think that the life of a young widow today is as hard as it was in ancient times?

26. Read Ruth 1:6–18. The widows Ruth, Naomi, and Orpah were faced with a severe famine. In a passage often quoted at weddings, how did Ruth express her love for Naomi and for Naomi's God (vv. 16–17)?

27. Read Ruth 1:19–2:2. What was Ruth determined to do for her mother-in-law (v. 2)? What lesson can we learn from Ruth about our relationships with in-laws and other family members?

Ruth, the Gleaner

Read Ruth 2:3–16. Ruth proved that she was unashamed to work hard for a living. God rewarded her faithfulness to her mother-in-law, Naomi, through a man named Boaz (BO-az).

28. Why did Boaz take a special interest in this poor foreigner (vv. 5–7)? Whom did he acknowledge as caring for her (v. 12)? How did Boaz encourage and help Ruth (vv. 14–16)?

29. Read Ruth 2:17–23. Why was Naomi happy that Ruth had found a good friend in Boaz?

Ruth's Remarkable Marriage

Read Ruth 3:1–18. Out of love and concern for her daughter-in-law, Naomi desired that Ruth remarry. Her suggestion for Ruth's nocturnal visit to Boaz was proper and effective.

30. How did Ruth and Boaz conduct themselves at this meeting? What promise did he make to her (vv. 10–13)? How did Boaz show his remarkable kindness (vv. 14–15)?

31. Read Ruth 4:1–13. Boaz had to offer a closer relative the opportunity to marry Ruth. How did he finally obtain the legal right to marry her (vv. 5–10)? How did Boaz demonstrate that he would be a virtuous husband (see Ephesians 5:25–33)?

32. What does the Bible tell us about the marriage and the happiness of this couple (4:13)? Besides the gift of children, what are other blessings of marriage?

33. Read vv. 14–22. What high honor did God bestow upon Ruth? How does Ruth's story encourage you to share your faith in Ruth's greatest descendant, Jesus Christ?

Other Women in Ruth's Time

34. Ruth's sister-in-law, Orpah, could have shared in Ruth's good fortune but failed to grasp the opportunity. What course did she prefer to take (Ruth 1:6–15)?

35. How did Naomi give evidence of a God-given faith? Why was she most happy when Ruth's child, Obed, was born (4:14–17)?

36. What interest did the women of Bethlehem show in Naomi and Ruth (Ruth 1:19; 4:14–17)? What are some ways Christian women might serve women of the world?

Closing Worship

Close by reading or singing together the words of "Go, My Children, with My Blessing" (*LSB* 922; *CW* 332).

Go, My children, with My blessing, Never alone.
Waking, sleeping, I am with you; You are My own.
   In my love's baptismal river
      I have made you Mine forever.
Go, My children, with My blessing—You are My own.

Go, My children, sins forgiven, At peace and pure.
Here you learned how much I love you, What I can cure.
   Here you heard My dear Son's story;
      Here you touched Him, saw His glory.
Go, My children, sins forgiven, At peace and pure.

Go, My children, fed and nourished, Closer to Me;
Grow in love and love by serving, Joyful and free.
   Here My Spirit's power filled you;
      Here His tender comfort stilled you.
Go, My children, fed and nourished, Joyful and free.

I the Lord will bless and keep you And give you peace;
I the Lord will smile upon you And give you peace:
   I the Lord will be your Father,
      Savior, Comforter, and Brother.
Go, My children; I will keep you And give you peace.

Jaroslav J. Vajda, b. 1919
© 1983 Concordia Publishing House

For Daily Bible Reading

Monday: Ruth 1
Tuesday: Ruth 2
Wednesday: Ruth 3
Thursday: Ruth 4
Friday: Proverbs 5
Saturday: 1 Corinthians 7
Sunday: Psalm 127; 128
For memorization: Ruth 1:16–17; Ecclesiastes 9:9;
Hebrews 13:16

%

Hannah

How great, beautiful, and precious is a mother's love! The story of Hannah and Samuel shows us that a pious and loving mother is one of the greatest gifts that God can give us in this life. Hannah shows us how much we owe to our mothers. In Hannah, the Bible painted one of its most beautiful pictures of a great woman. Should we be surprised that the Bible, which normally details both the good and bad in the lives of its characters, describes no flaw in Samuel's personality? That is because Hannah's noble character was through her love and attention faithfully reproduced in her son.

Hannah, a Woman of Prayer and Faith

Hannah was one of Elkanah's (el-KAH-nuh) two wives. Elkanah was a righteous man who sacrificed to the Lord at Shiloh and showed double mercy to his beloved wife, Hannah (1 Samuel 1).

37. In spite of what we may presume was a happy home, why was Hannah miserable (vv. 2–8)?

38. How did Hannah show that God had given her a strong faith (vv. 9–18)? How does Hannah's persistent prayer serve as a model for all Christians (see also 1 Thessalonians 5:17)?

39. Discuss Hannah's vow (v. 11). When do Christian parents dedicate, or consecrate, their children to God?

Hannah, a Woman Who Kept Her Promise

By God's grace, Hannah conceived and gave birth to a son, Samuel (vv. 19–20). God had heard and answered her prayer.

40. What does God promise about prayer (see Mark 11:24; John 16:23; James 1:5–7; 1 John 5:14)? What should we do if God seemingly does not grant our requests (Luke 18:1)?

41. Was Hannah sorry that she had made this vow to the Lord (v. 28)? Besides religious upbringing, what other important decisions do parents make for their infants and children?

42. Read 1 Samuel 2:18–21. How did Hannah continue to exert a positive influence upon her son after he was away from home? Discuss ways you can provide a positive influence upon family members and friends.

Hannah's Hymn of Praise and Thanksgiving

God's answer to Hannah's prayer evoked a wonderful hymn of praise and thanksgiving (1 Samuel 2:1–10). However, the chief reason for Hannah's joyful mood was the Lord's salvation (v. 1).

43. What warning does Hannah give to people who do not put their trust in God and pray to Him (vv. 3–10)? How does her hymn give testimony to her faith in Christ ("His anointed" [v. 10])?

44. Read Luke 1:46–55. Note the resemblance between Hannah's hymn and Mary's Magnificat. If you feel comfortable, share when you have offered a spontaneous hymn of praise to the Lord.

Other Women in Hannah's Time

45. Who was the other wife of Hannah's husband, Elkanah (1 Samuel 1:2–7)? In what ways can you be a blessing to others in spite of difficult or unusual circumstances?

46. The wife of Phinehas (fi-NAY-us) grieved over the capture of the ark of the covenant and the deaths of her father-in-law and husband (1 Samuel 4:19–22). What do her last words indicate about her faith?

47. What sadness must have accompanied Samuel's wife concerning their children (1 Samuel 8:1–5)? How can your congregation minister to people facing unique challenges in their families?

48. King Saul disobeyed the Lord by consulting a wicked woman for advice (1 Samuel 28). Why should Christians rely only on the strength of God's Word?

Closing Worship

Close by reading or singing together the words of "The King of Love My Shepherd Is" (*LSB* 709; *LW* 412; *TLH* 431; *LBW* 456; *CW* 375; *ELH* 370).

The King of love my shepherd is,
  Whose goodness faileth never;
I nothing lack if I am His
  And He is mine forever.

Where streams of living water flow,
  My ransomed soul He leadeth
And, where the verdant pastures grow,
  With food celestial feedeth.

Perverse and foolish oft I strayed,
  But yet in love He sought me
And on His shoulder gently laid
  And home rejoicing brought me.

In death's dark vale I fear no ill
  With Thee, dear Lord, beside me,
Thy rod and staff my comfort still,
  Thy cross before to guide me.

Thou spreadst a table in my sight;
  Thine unction grace bestoweth;
And, oh, what transport of delight
  From Thy pure chalice floweth!

And so through all the length of days
  Thy goodness faileth never;
Good Shepherd, may I sing Thy praise
  Within Thy house forever!

Henry W. Baker, 1821–77
Public domain

For Daily Bible Reading

Monday: 1 Samuel 1
Tuesday: 1 Samuel 2
Wednesday: 1 Samuel 3–4
Thursday: 1 Samuel 5–7
Friday: 1 Samuel 8–10
Saturday: 1 Samuel 28
Sunday: Job 1:1–2:10
For memorization: Job 1:21b; 2:10; 1 Samuel 2:7;
2 Timothy 1:5

Leader Guide

Each one-hour session is divided into three to six subsections. Participants will first look at the life of the historical figure in the biblical text. Then they will be encouraged from what they read and discuss to make practical application to their own lives and situations.

Remember that this study is only a guide. Your role as group leader is to facilitate interaction between individual participants and the biblical text and between participants in your small group. By God's Spirit working through His Word, participants will learn and grow together.

Begin and end each session with prayer. Each session concludes with suggestions for weekly Bible readings, Bible memorization, and a hymn. You may choose a different hymn or song based on the needs of your group.

Jochebed and Miriam

Moses was one of the greatest men in history, and many participants may be well acquainted with his story in the Bible. However, our purpose is to study the great women who played important and influential roles in his life. No fewer than four women contributed to his development: his mother, Jochebed; his sister, Miriam; the daughter of Pharaoh; and his wife, Zipporah. This session considers primarily the first two women, who undoubtedly contributed the most to the making of Moses.

Jochebed, a Loving and Resourceful Mother

In giving their daughter the name *Jochebed* (Hebrew: "The LORD is glory"), Jochebed's parents showed how highly they loved and honored God. The Bible doesn't mention the name of Moses' mother until Exodus 6:20. She was a daughter of Levi, the son of Leah (Exodus 2:1). She married her nephew Amram (such marriages were later forbidden [Leviticus 18:12]).

1. In addition to Moses, Jochebed's two other children were Miriam and Aaron. Aaron was about three years older than Moses, and Miriam was probably five or more years older than Aaron, so Moses was the baby of the family.

2. Most participants will be familiar with the story of baby Moses. We have here one of the most remarkable examples of a mother's love. Jochebed risked her life by hiding Moses as long as she could. When this was no longer possible, she carefully devised another plan. By setting her child in a basket among the reeds that grew along the Nile River in Egypt, she showed both her resourcefulness and her strong, God-given faith (see Hebrews 11:23).

This act places Jochebed in the forefront of all mothers in history. Undoubtedly, Jochebed discovered the time when Pharaoh's daughter took her regular bath at the Nile and planned to appeal to the princess's sympathy. If she showed interest in Moses, his life would be saved.

3. God rewarded Jochebed for putting her trust in Him. Clearly, the Lord orchestrated all these events because Moses was to become one of His greatest servants. Jochebed carefully instructed her daughter, Miriam, in the role she was to play in saving the youngest member of their family and entrusted her with this solemn responsibility.

What if Moses had grown up only in Pharaoh's court without coming under the influence of his godly mother? Perhaps he would have remained only a pagan prince. As a youth, Moses would live in the court to learn the wisdom and ways of the Egyptians. But his mother, who foresaw the dangers to which he would be exposed, faithfully implanted God's Word in his young heart so that his later experiences could not ruin his faith (see Hebrews 11:24–26). Jochebed serves as a model to all Christian mothers, grandmothers, aunts, and other family members and friends to take every opportunity to teach God's Word to children (see Proverbs 22:6; 2 Timothy 1:5; 3:14–15).

Miriam, a Leader of Women

4. As a young girl of eight or ten years, Miriam proved to be dependable and intelligent, obedient to her parents, and concerned about the welfare of her baby brother. We can imagine how lovingly she watched over her little brother and helped her mother care for him. Who can estimate the influence she had upon him as a child and youth!

5. Miriam must have been about ninety years old at the time of the Exodus (see Exodus 7:7.) The Bible doesn't indicate if she ever married or if she had children. God appointed all three of Jochebed's children as leaders of the children of Israel, including Miriam (Micah 6:4). In Exodus 15:20, she is called a "prophetess," which means that God may have given her a special gift to receive and interpret special revelations from Him. It could also mean that God designated her as a teacher of women. She is pictured as the leader of the Hebrew women in Exodus 15:20.

But she was also a gifted musician and poetess. She composed the brief poem in v. 21, which was probably the chief thought or refrain of a longer hymn. Some think she also composed the hymn in vv. 1–19. Miriam is the first choir leader mentioned in the Bible.

Miriam serves as an example of a woman who dedicated her life and work to God's glory and who served the welfare of her people.

If they feel comfortable, encourage participants to share the gifts they believe God has given them to serve others. Some participants may feel most comfortable having others in the group do this for them. For example, "I am thankful that Susan took the time last week to pray with me," or, "Luz, I'm grateful that you are such an encouraging person."

6. Numbers 12 describes an incident where Miriam (and Aaron) became jealous of Moses and his authority among God's people. God disciplined Miriam for her disobedience by giving her a skin disease, which meant she had to spend time outside of the camp of Israel. Because of the prayers of Moses and the people, the Lord relieved her suffering after a week by fully restoring her health.

This incident teaches us the importance of recognizing not only our gifts and God-given responsibilities but also the gifts and responsibilities of others. Read 1 Corinthians 12:21–26, and allow participants to discuss the importance of affirming and supporting our gifts and the gifts and responsibilities of other believers.

Other Women of That Period

7. The midwives in this passage feared God more than they did mighty Pharaoh. When it comes to choosing between obeying an earthly authority and what God says to us in His Word, we must choose the latter. Allow participants to suggest contemporary examples of this apparent conflict in our lives today. One example is being asked to perform an illegal activity at the workplace.

8. Despite his horrible order (Exodus 1:22), Pharaoh's daughter seems to have been kind and compassionate to the Hebrews, who to the Egyptians were a foreign culture and race. No doubt she knew of her father's edict but desired to save this Hebrew baby in spite of it. Through Pharaoh's daughter, God saved Moses by drawing him out of the water (2:10). As an adult, God would use Moses to save God's people through the waters of the Red Sea (Exodus 14:13–31).

9. Although he was a great servant of God, Moses was not beyond sin and not beyond needing the help of the great women in his

life. Exodus 4 shows how mighty Moses was sometimes meek and had a weak faith. Undoubtedly this frustrated the Lord, for He became angry with Moses (Exodus 4:14). Moses also had not maintained the covenant by having His son circumcised (see Genesis 17:9–14). But God preserved Moses' life through his wife, Zipporah, who performed the rite herself. Without her faithful intervention, God would have destroyed His servant Moses.

Allow participants to discuss the important spiritual role wives have in service to their husbands, including prayer, supporting his role as the head of the household, and, when necessary, rebuke.

10. Note that both women and men brought together all of the required materials for the construction of the tabernacle, the place of God's presence and the sacrifices for sin. In addition to the creation of worship materials (threads and yarns, precious metals, precious and semiprecious stones, fragrant spices and oils, animal skins, etc.), women may have been involved in their acquisition and disbursement. Keep in mind that this was a tremendous undertaking that took skill and finesse, especially given that the Hebrews were now refugees traveling right into a desert. What courage and faith!

Allow participants to discuss what opportunities for service in your congregation are available for women.

11. The daughters of Zelophehad, Mahlah, Noah, Hoglah, Milcah, and Tirzah, approached the Tent of Meeting in the presence of Moses, Eleazar the priest, and other leaders and pressed their case for financial equality. Moses, in turn, inquired of the Lord, and the Lord granted their request. This serves as an example of pursuing a legitimate complaint for fair treatment and following the proper channels to have that complaint resolved.

Allow participants to discuss the ways Christians can pursue fair treatment through the appropriate means and channels.

12. Rahab was a prostitute in Jericho whose home made up part of the city wall (Joshua 2:1, 15). She was a legal ancestress of Christ (Matthew 1:1, 5). Through faith she believed in God (Joshua 2:8–13; Hebrews 11:31) and aided the Hebrew spies (see Joshua 2). Her God-given faith enabled her outward righteousness of good works (James 2:25). Rahab, a sinner saved by God's grace, is a model of what God can do with even the worst of sinners.

Allow participants to discuss how the Gospel of God's grace in Christ can and does liberate us to become all that God has called us to be (Galatians 3:26–27; Ephesians 2:8–10; Hebrews 12:1–2).

Deborah

In our previous session we looked at Jochebed, Moses' brave and faithful mother, and at his sister, Miriam, who became a great leader of women during the period of the Exodus and beyond. In this session we will meet a woman whom God appointed to lead His people by serving as a judge in Israel. Her leadership was not simply over women, however. She also led men. This great woman was also one of the few women whom the Bible calls prophetess. What was it about Deborah that makes her a great woman of the Bible?

Deborah as a Judge

To understand Deborah, we need to know something about the time in which she lived. The first three chapters of the Book of Judges help us here. After Joshua' death, Israel was without a strong leader. The people became corrupt through idolatry (Judges 2:8–15). God punished them by permitting heathen nations to rule over them (vv. 14–15, 19–22 and following). These unhappy conditions continued for about three hundred years. Whenever the Israelites repented and prayed to God for help, the Lord sent them judges to help them drive out their enemies. Deborah was one of these judges.

13. At the time of our story, a strong Canaanite confederacy had cruelly oppressed the Israelites for twenty years. Sisera, the commanding general of the Canaanite army, was greatly feared not only because of his power and success but also because he was a brutal tyrant. By depriving the Israelites of their weapons and re-sources, he had made it almost impossible for them to revolt or to defend themselves (5:8). They had lost all hope and courage. To restore these was Deborah's first task.

14. Deborah was a married woman. However, we are not told whether her husband, Lappidoth, was still living. Deborah was so well-known and honored that the place where she lived was called after her name (Judges 4:4–5). The Lord had given to her the gift of

prophecy, by which she could reveal God's will to the people. He had also appointed her to be a judge over His people, which gave her the right to decide cases and give orders. The men of Israel consulted her and sought her advice and judgment. Her home was between Ramah and Bethel, in the hills of Ephraim. She was a divinely approved ruler and was honored as "a mother in Israel" (Judges 5:7).

The Israelites needed a leader like the pious and energetic Deborah to lift their drooping spirits. She was a brave and resourceful woman but also one who trusted in God and acted according to His Word. She was forthright but collegial in her dealings with Barak, the commander of the Israelite army. She told him to take ten thousand men to the top of Mount Tabor and attack the huge Canaanite army. She assured him that God would give him a great victory (Judges 4:6–7). Barak hesitated to risk battle with Sisera unless Deborah accompanied him. He believed that only her presence would give his men courage to fight.

15. Deborah did not lead the army or take part in the fighting. She did, however, encourage the Israelites to engage in battle (4:14–15). Note the unequal size of the two armies (vv. 10–13). In answer to Deborah's prayer, God gave Barak a great victory. All of the Canaanites except Sisera, the commander of Canaanite King Jabin's army, died by the sword (v. 16); perhaps their dead bodies were swept away by the River Kishon (v. 13).

Jael's act for her nation must be judged in the light of the times. She was a descendant of Moses' father-in-law, some of whose people had joined the Israelites. There is a sense of irony here that God would use a "bee" (Deborah) and a "mountain goat" (Jael) to preserve the "land flowing with milk and honey" for His people (see Exodus 3:8, 17; Leviticus 20:24; Deuteronomy 6:3).

16. Deborah was a woman who feared and served God with the best of her abilities. She used her gifts and position to help her people. Allow participants to discuss Deborah's other godly traits that make her a good example of a woman who lived her life by faith.

Deborah's Hymn of Victory

Deborah and Barak's song of praise is directed not toward themselves or their abilities and accomplishments but to "the LORD, the God of Israel" (Judges 5:3). While God works through many people and events in order to bless us, our praise for both large and small blessings and victories should be directed toward Him.

17. Allow participants who feel comfortable doing so to share with the group the victories that God has won for them in their lives. The greatest battle over our greatest enemies—sin, death, and the devil—was won for us by Jesus on the cross. However, God provides other victories in our lives as well. Examples may include a victory over a particular temptation, a clean bill of health after treatment for cancer, a restored relationship with a son or daughter, a new job, the conversion and Baptism of an adult friend and her family, and so on.

18. Deborah praised Jael for her courageous deed (vv. 24–27) and rejoiced over the swift punishment that God had brought upon the enemies of His people (vv. 28–31). Just as Deborah highlighted her vocation as a "mother in Israel," so also did she mention that Jael was the "wife of Heber the Kenite" (v. 24). Deborah and Jael were extraordinary women doing extraordinary things in extraordinary times, and yet they did not disdain or diminish their God-given vocations as women.

Other Women in the Book of Judges

19. Achsah was the daughter of Caleb, one of those sent to explore the land of Canaan before the people of Israel entered it (Numbers 13:6). Just as Caleb was honorable and God-fearing (Deuteronomy 1:35–36), so, too, apparently was Achsah. Caleb gave Achsah to Othniel, Caleb's nephew, as a reward for capturing the city of Kiriath-sepher. Achsah respectfully asked her father for a blessing and received it. We, too, should be respectfully assertive in asking for what we need. We pray to our heavenly Father, "Give us this day our daily bread." Likewise, when we need help or assistance or are being denied basic goods in order to survive, we should

in confidence make our requests to those whom God has placed in our lives to assist us.

20. Jephthah made a rash vow to wholly consecrate whatever came out of his house first if he were victorious in battle over the Ammonites. While Jephthah promised to sacrifice a "burnt offering" (v. 31), it is unclear what his daughter's ultimate fate was. Many commentators find in this Bible passage a reason to believe that Jephthah "wholly consecrated" his daughter to a lifetime of celibacy: (a) she was an only child (v. 34); (b) she wept with her friends because she would never marry (v. 37); (c) Scripture notes that she was a virgin (v. 39). While we should be wary of making promises that we cannot fulfill, we should be especially wary of making promises to God that we cannot keep or will later come to regret. Jesus says, "And do not take an oath by your head, for you cannot make one hair white or black. Let what you say be simply 'Yes' or 'no'; anything more than this comes from evil" (Matthew 5:36–37).

21. Manoah and his wife were the parents of Samson. The Angel of the Lord first appeared to Manoah's wife (Judges 13:3), who was unable to conceive, similar to the appearance of the angel Gabriel to the Virgin Mary (see Luke 1:26–28). In this passage, the Angel of the Lord appearing to her was the pre-incarnate Christ (compare Judges 13:18 with Isaiah 9:6). When Manoah realized that this Angel was God, he was struck with fear (Judges 13:22). However, filled with faith, his wife gave him courage (v. 23). Allow participants to discuss when God strengthened their faith for a special task.

22. God moved Samson to desire marriage with a Philistine woman because He planned to work on behalf of His people (Judges 14:4). Although Samson may not have known it, he was acting according to God's will in this particular matter. As Christians, we should be more concerned about God's will for our lives, recorded in the Scriptures, than the opinions of others. Allow participants to discuss practical applications of that in their lives.

23. Most participants will be familiar with the story of Samson and Delilah. Delilah agreed to help the Philistines by seductively gaining his confidence in order to discover the true secret of his strength. Ultimately, it was unbelief (Judges 16:20), not a shaved head, that led to Samson's undoing. By violating the covenant into

which he had been born, he proved that his temporal pleasure was more important to him than his eternal destiny. Participants may want to read the rest of the story (vv. 22–31), which shows that Samson returned to faith and performed a mighty deed for the Lord at the time of his death.

24. Micah's mother was a syncretist, that is, she mixed the worship of the one true God with that of pagan idols. Some parents do that today as well, mixing the worship of the Holy Trinity with occult practices, such as Ouija boards and horoscopes, or mixing beliefs, such as combining Christianity with Hinduism (believing that Jesus is divine and believing in reincarnation). In any case, Christians are not absolved of their duties of respect, support, and love for their parents, regardless of whether they are faithful Christians or not (1 Timothy 5:4). Christians should pray for all of their relatives, including their parents, so that if they do not yet believe they will come to faith and if they do believe their faith will be strengthened in Jesus Christ, the friend of sinners.

Ruth

Probably no other book of the Bible has appealed so strongly to the general public and to the literary world as the Book of Ruth. Samuel Johnson, the celebrated English author, once proposed to tell a story to some distinguished members of a literary club. Without telling them that the story was from the Bible, he read them the story of Ruth. The members were delighted with its simplicity and the personal strength of its heroine. They were eager to learn the name of the author, who, they all agreed, could grace any circle of literature.

Ruth's Loyalty to Naomi

The Book of Judges portrays moral and spiritual conditions during the time of Ruth, about sixty years before the birth of David. Ruth's people, the Moabites, lived east of the Dead Sea. While descendants of Lot (Genesis 19:36–37) and thus distantly related to Israel, the Moabites were also idolaters (see also Deuteronomy 23:3–6). By living in a heathen land and intermarrying with unbelievers, Naomi's family subjected itself to grave spiritual dangers. However, Naomi's piety and energetic witness probably influenced her Gentile daughters-in-law to adopt the Hebrew religion.

25. In addition to being widowed, Naomi, Orpah, and Ruth also seem to have been without material means to support themselves. The lot of poor widows in ancient times was pitiful beyond description.

Allow participants to discuss the plight of modern widows (and widowers) today. In what ways are their lives comparable to people in Ruth's day? In what ways are they different? What can churches today do to relieve the suffering of widows and widowers and their children?

26. Ruth loved her mother-in-law, Naomi, and had evidently also considered what it would mean to remain alone in a heathen country without her. Ruth's attachment and devotion to Naomi is remarkable. Her conversion to the one true God had resulted in a

complete change of her heart. She pledged her life to Naomi and to Naomi's God (Ruth 1:16–17). Such love and devotion is the work of the Holy Spirit, enabled through the Gospel.

27. Living before the prophet Micah, Ruth and Naomi would not have known that Bethlehem would be the birthplace of the Savior (see Micah 5:2). The women of the town eyed the newcomers at first with curiosity, but when they learned how poor Naomi was, they lost all interest in her and Ruth. In Bethlehem, the two women were left to their own resources. Naomi became discouraged and bitter, but Ruth did her best to cheer and support her. She was neither ashamed of her mother-in-law nor of earning her living by hard labor.

Allow participants to discuss what lessons we may learn from Ruth, especially regarding our in-laws and other family members.

Ruth, the Gleaner

28. Ruth was not afraid of hard work. She supported herself and her mother-in-law cheerfully. The Law forbade landowners to reap the grain that stood in the corners of their fields and the stalks that had been dropped by the reapers. The gleanings were to be left to the poor (see Leviticus 19:9–10). Barley, harvested in April, was the fare of the poor. God led Ruth to the fields of Boaz, a God-fearing, kind, generous, and respected man. We might think that Boaz was first attracted to Ruth because of her looks, but her diligent work is what caught his eye (vv. 5–7). Like Ruth, Boaz was a person of faith—he recognized that God had brought Ruth to his fields to bless her, and he eagerly desired to participate in God's blessing of Ruth (v. 12). Boaz honored Ruth for her loyalty, virtue, and piety and helped her generously (vv. 14–16).

29. Ruth's reports to Naomi show how deeply she trusted her mother-in-law and how much she appreciated her wise counsel. Naomi recognized the name of Boaz as that of a relative and saw not merely an opportunity to improve their immediate fortunes but also a possibility of arranging marriage between him and Ruth. Naomi was truly concerned about Ruth's long-term well-being.

Ruth's Remarkable Marriage

30. Today we might question whether or not such an evening as proposed by Naomi might be advantageous or even proper. However, Boaz and Ruth displayed proper and legitimate behavior in their circumstances at that time. God Himself had provided for the care of widows by establishing the Mosaic law of the levirate marriage (Deuteronomy 25:5–10). Naomi merely took advantage of the provisions of that law. According to this law, if a man died without leaving children, it was the duty of his brother or nearest relative to marry his widow. Naomi wished to remind Boaz of this duty. Custom allowed women the right to make this request. Divine providence prepared the way and brought Ruth and Boaz together in a chaste, orderly manner. Boaz promised Ruth that he would undertake the levirate marriage if Naomi's nearest relative would not do it (Ruth 3:10–13). Not only did he display concern for her reputation, although she had done nothing wrong, Boaz also generously provided for Ruth and Naomi's physical needs (vv. 14–15).

31. Ruth's marriage was conducted and concluded according to God's will. Another relative, who stood closer to Naomi, did not feel he was in a position to marry Ruth; therefore, he publicly renounced his right to acquire what property Naomi had. The shoe signified possession, since a man walked over the land that belonged to him. By taking off his shoe and handing it to another person, Naomi's relative renounced all claim to the property and rights in question. Having settled the matter in court, Boaz took Ruth to be his wife (4:5–10). Throughout their relationship recorded in the Book of Ruth, Boaz, through his concern for her well-being, his generosity, and so forth serves as a good model for husbands.

Allow participants to read Ephesians 5:25–33 to see how our divine Husband, Jesus Christ, serves us, His Bride, the Church.

32. The words describing Ruth's second marriage, to Boaz, are few but significant (Ruth 4:13). Ruth was thus officially adopted into the Hebrew nation as a member of God's chosen people. The birth of a son, Obed (the grandfather of David, v. 17), brought joy and comfort into the life of aging Naomi. Ruth was not the first Gentile woman to become a celebrated mother in Israel. Boaz's own mother was Rahab. The chief purpose of the story of Ruth is to

show how a Gentile woman became the great-grandmother of David. Children are a "heritage from the LORD" (Psalm 127:3). Allow participants to discuss other blessings and benefits of marriage.

33. God blessed Ruth by allowing her to become the grandmother of David (vv. 14–22) and, ultimately, an ancestress of Christ (see also Matthew 1:5–6, 16). By numbering Gentiles among His ancestors, Christ wished to indicate that He was the Savior of all people and that the Gentiles are also to be brought into His Church (see also Isaiah 49:6; Luke 2:30–32).

Allow participants to select aspects of Ruth's story that are applicable to their own lives and then discuss how her story and theirs can help them to share their faith in Ruth's greatest descendant, Jesus Christ.

Other Women in Ruth's Time

34. Orpah was a person who found it easy to express her love in words but was too weak to prove it with deeds. She went back to her home and her gods.

35. Participants may enjoy spending some time discussing Naomi's faith and the love that she showed to Ruth. She is undoubtedly one of the great women in the history of the Church. Without the example and guidance of Naomi, Ruth would have remained unknown to the people of God. Although Naomi became discouraged through poverty and widowhood, we shouldn't believe that she lost her faith. The birth of Obed gave her great joy because she knew that her family line and the line of her deceased husband would be preserved through him.

36. The women of Bethlehem recognized that God had blessed Naomi by giving Ruth a husband, securing their future, providing for their well-being, and preserving their family through the birth of Obed.

Allow participants to discuss ways today's Christian women might serve other women of the world in their spiritual and temporal needs.

Hannah

The Bible impartially relays the facts about great women and men. It truthfully points out their many faults just as it extols their many virtues. However, the story of Hannah and Samuel is different. We find nothing in the Scriptures that casts a shadow upon the character of Hannah and Samuel. Of course, they were sinners, just like the rest of us. However, the Bible highlights only their good qualities, lives lived by the power of the Holy Spirit working through the Gospel.

Hannah, a Woman of Prayer and Faith

37. Hannah's name means "charm, grace, beauty." She is an example of a woman who trusted in the Lord and placed herself entirely in His hand for guidance. The fact that she was childless made her unhappy. As we've noted before, women in ancient times regarded their childlessness as a curse. Because the Lord seemingly had turned from Hannah in disfavor, she suffered the constant annoyances and taunts of her rival, Peninnah (vv. 6–7).

38. Although Hannah had to suffer under a heavy cross, she did not complain, nor did she show any jealousy or hatred toward Peninnah. Patiently she bore her grief in her heart and trusted in God to help her. She did not refuse to accompany her husband to Shiloh and participate in the religious services there, even though at such times she felt her loneliness and sorrow most keenly. She knew that only God could relieve her of her cross. Therefore, she went into the house of God and poured out her heart to the Lord in fervent prayer. Only a strong faith persists in deep and soulful prayer; indeed, "What a friend we have in Jesus, All our sins and griefs to bear! What a privilege to carry Ev'rything to God in prayer! Oh, what peace we often forfeit; Oh, what needless pain we bear—All because we do not carry Ev'rything to God in prayer!"

Hannah's persistent prayer, like the prayer of the persistent widow (see Luke 18:1–8), is a model for all Christians. We should, as Paul says, "pray without ceasing" (1 Thessalonians 5:17).

39. Hannah was so sincere and unselfish in her prayer that she vowed to give back to God as a thank-offering the very thing she was asking of Him. She promised to dedicate her son to the Lord to be His minister. She was willing to give Him what her heart craved the most; by giving her best she gave herself.

Christian parents dedicate, or consecrate, their children to God when they bring them to Him to be born again in Holy Baptism, give them Christian instruction and training in the home, and use the educational facilities of the church to prepare them for confirmation and full church membership. They give their children to God in a special way when they help them become pastors, missionaries, or teachers in church schools.

Hannah, a Woman Who Kept Her Promise

40. Hannah was not only comforted, but in a short time she also had God's answer to her prayer. Within a year she became a mother. God granted her petition at once because it was a wholly unselfish request and because through her He wanted to bless the whole Hebrew nation. Are our prayers always like Hannah's prayer, so that God can grant them without harming us?

Allow participants to look up the Bible promises about prayer. In the prayer of the persistent widow (see question and answer 38), Jesus says that we "ought always to pray and not lose heart" (Luke 18:1). Perhaps participants would like to share how their prayer lives were strengthened and encouraged by the faith and good words of other believers.

41. Hannah expressed her faith in God by calling her child Samuel ("heard of God"). She loved Samuel and would gladly have kept him. But even though no one except God had heard her make her vow, she was bound to keep her promise. The longer she waited, the harder it would be for her to give up her son into the Lord's service. Hannah clearly did not regret her vow or her decision to keep it (v. 28), even though Samuel was still very young (Hebrew women weaned their children at the age of three).

Parents make many decisions on behalf of their children. The point of this question is to clarify that decisions regarding the religious upbringing of children are no different; such decisions should not be left to chance or left up to the child when he or she gets older.

42. Once a year, Hannah went to Shiloh to visit Samuel, each time bringing him a new coat, into which she had no doubt stitched many a prayer for her son (2:19). Samuel certainly never forgot his mother, and he profited by her influence all his life. We see this by looking at his character and from the fact that later as a man he made his home at Ramah.

Allow participants to discuss the ways they can continue to have a godly influence on distant family members, children who've gone off to college, friends who've moved away, and others.

Hannah's Hymn of Praise and Thanksgiving

43. Hannah's hymn (1 Samuel 2:1–10) should be read and discussed for its content and poetic beauty. Hannah warns against spiritual pride and arrogance, which are useless and are crushed under the weight of God's holiness, wisdom, and perfection (v. 3). Hannah's hymn reaches its climax in verse 10, ending in a confession of her faith in the promised Messiah, the Lord's "anointed."

44. Compare Hannah's hymn (1 Samuel 2:1–10) to Mary's Magnificat (Luke 1:46–55). Both hymns follow very much the same line of thought and move in the language and spirit of the Psalms. Mary was probably very familiar with Hannah's hymn and other portions of the Old Testament Scriptures.

Allow participants to discuss when, like Hannah and Mary, they were overjoyed with the Lord's work in their lives and offered a spontaneous hymn of praise.

Other Women in Hannah's Time

45. Elkanah's other wife was Peninnah (puh-NEE-nuh), who had many children by Elkanah (1 Samuel 1:4). Instead of helping and comforting Hannah in her childlessness, Peninnah chose to cause Hannah additional anguish (vv. 6–7). Undoubtedly, this was a difficult situation for Hannah.

Allow participants to discuss ways that they can be a blessing to others in the midst of their need or suffering. Childlessness can be one of many examples.

46. The wife of Phinehas, the daughter-in-law of Eli, grieved because of the death of her husband and father-in-law. Before she died in childbirth, she gave her son the name *Ichabod*, which means "no glory," because the "glory had departed" with the capture of the ark of the covenant, the location of God's special presence on earth. While ending on a sad note, her words do indicate faith in the promises God had made with His covenant people, which were illustrated by the presence of the ark among them.

47. Unlike Samuel and, most likely, his wife, their sons, Joel and Abijah, were morally corrupt. Perhaps you or someone in your group can relate to the disappointment parents sometimes experience when it comes to the choices their daughters or sons make in their lives.

Allow participants to discuss what practical ways members can minister to people facing difficulties in marital and parent-child relationships, as well as in other areas.

48. Although not a "great woman," the witch of Endor influenced Saul by conjuring the spirit of Samuel. Perhaps God allowed an evil spirit, or demon, to appear to the woman and to the king in the form of Samuel; we do not know. Nevertheless, the prediction (1 Samuel 28:19) came true: both Saul and his sons would die the next day (31:1–6).

Allow participants to discuss the dangers of consulting mediums, fortune tellers, horoscopes, and so on (see Leviticus 19:31; Deuteronomy 18:10–12; Ecclesiastes 7:14). Instead of these, Christians should seek help from the Lord (John 16:23) and rely on His Word (Isaiah 66:2; Colossians 3:16).

CPSIA information can be obtained
at www.ICGtesting.com
Printed in the USA
LVOW13s0328230218
567473LV00009B/70/P